The Other Pulpit

Life Lessons of a Leader!

Pastor Steve L. Turner

Order this book online at www.trafford.com
or email orders@trafford.com

Most Trafford titles are also available at major online book retailers.

Printed in the United States of America.

ISBN: 978-1-4907-3329-6 (sc)
ISBN: 978-1-4907-3330-2 (hc)
ISBN: 978-1-4907-3331-9 (e)

Library of Congress Control Number: 2014908093

Trafford rev. 08/05/2014

www.trafford.com

North America & international
toll-free: 1 888 232 4444 (USA & Canada)
fax: 812 355 4082

Contents

Contents

THE AUTHOR HAS BEEN IN MUSIC TRAINING SINCE AGE 4.

HE HAS BEEN PLAYING MUSIC FOR OVER 40 YEARS.

HE HAS BEEN A MINISTER OF MUSIC FOR 34 YEARS.

HE HAS PROMOTED GOSPEL MUSIC CONCERTS FOR 17 YEARS.

HE BELIEVES THAT GOSPEL MUSIC SHOULD GO BEYOND THE CHURCH WALLS, AND HE HAS TAKEN IT TO CORPORATE AMERICA.

My Other Brother

Testimonial

Hi, I am Pastor Walter A. Simms, a friend and brother in the Lord to Pastor Steve Turner. I first met Pastor Turner several years ago thru my older sister who he managed and coached in a musical group of three women called, The Voices. In 2006 I started working with my bishop and learning to take over duties at my home church, which included planning church services and events. I started to call on Steve to help provide the music at many of our important services and fundraisers. He has been a tremendous help in times when we needed a musician to fill in right away. He is a constant professional who gives more than music when he is working for the Lord, he gives himself, and you can feel his commitment in every song he sings.

Pastor Turner started teaching two of the young teenagers at my church to play the keyboard and they have been growing in their knowledge of music. My hope is that they will not only keep playing to the glory of God, but that music may open doors for them in the future; maybe a music scholarship. When the mother of the church went home to be with the Lord, Pastor Turner helped us give her a home going service that will be remembered for years.

He is more than a musician and more than a friend, he is family. I have two natural brothers and one or two brothers in the Lord that

I have adopted; Pastor Turner is one of them. We find ourselves texting and calling each other to talk about our daily happenings or to agree in prayer for love ones, friends, and church members. We as pastors also need to hear words of encouragement now and then. In times of trouble we have been there for each other to hold up our hands to God and unite until we get victory.

I am what you may call an old soul, and some call a hell fire and brimstone preacher, but I don't deviate from the teaching of the Bible. Some contemporary music and forms of entertainment I do not agree with, but Pastor Turner has always respected my stand on the Word of God. I have understood Pastor Turner when others have not. Some try to figure him out, but the Spirit of God which is a discerner of the thoughts and the intent of the heart has given me that gift so that I see a man devoted to God, family, and his love for music. Brother Turner is a man that loves to worship and praise God. I call him brother because I know he would not mind, to show that he is also a humble man.

One of the best things you can do is take some time and get to know my other brother.

God bless you,

Pastor Walter A. Simms

Christ Like Church of God Apostolic

THIS BOOK IS DEDICATED TO THE ANGELS THAT GOD SURROUNDED ME WITH TO DEVELOP MY CALLING AND SPIRITUAL GIFTS.

MOST NOTABLY MY MOTHER WHO NOW RESIDES IN HEAVEN. SHE WAS AN UNTIRING MOTIVATOR OF EXCELLENCE.

MY CLASSICAL MUSIC INSTRUCTOR FOR 11 YEARS.

MY GOSPEL MUSIC INSTRUCTOR WHO TAUGHT ME PIANO / HAMMOND B3 / VOICE.

They are not alive to see their finished works but their legacy of love lives on within me.

- SPECIAL THANKS TO EAST GATE MINISTRIES
- SPECIAL THANKS TO PASTOR WALTER SIMMS
- SPECIAL THANKS TO DESIGNS BY NHEA
- SPECIAL THANKS TO MY WIFE WHOSE SUPPORT IS PRICELESS.
- SPECIAL THANKS TO MARIA MORALES, CEO OF RICANA PR. FOR EDITING SERVICES.
- SPECIAL THANKS TO YOU FOR PURCHASING THIS BOOK.
- SPECIAL THANKS TO MY STAFF OF VOLUNTEERS
- SPECIAL THANKS TO MY BROTHER FOR HIS COURAGE.
- ALL PRAISES TO GOD

Doctor Amanda Williams,
Pastor of the Mt. Calvary Holy Temple.

- In memory of my godparents, Bishop Harold Ivory and Aunt Amanda Williams, who were instrumental in my music ministry development. He trained my mother's choir and she allowed me to be trained by Sis. Mattie," her minister of music during Sunday Services.

- Elder Mark and Hope Mason, their son-in-law and daughter—her for her lifelong support and showing me what a real praise and worship team was all about; and he for leaving a church service to find me when I had been rejected and encouraging me to never give up, after I'd vowed to God that I would never play again.

THE OTHER PULPIT

Prelude / Intro

This inspired writing, long overdue, is released to liberate not only myself, but a hidden nation of forgotten and discarded lost offspring of illicit relationships and affairs. Unable to be raised in the same home, we for whatever reason were "left behind." Subsequently, as great cathedrals and dynasties were created for their first families and other favored cliques, we were outcasted as spiritual lepers. Recipients of only partial love, attention and financial support—or none at all—we, like casualties of war, were left for dead. As a "Pastor's Kid", given only fragmented stolen moments with my father, I apparently was not important enough to have his parental presence at my birthdays, graduations and other hallmark events. My mother was left to answer my questions, and to console my pain, and the emptiness of incompleteness. Are we the illegitimate offspring of God's anointed, no less leaders? Are we not destined to represent God both in and outside the church? Would God use "spiritual bio-hazard waste" to promote His kingdom? There is a great cloud of witnesses, who are the sons and daughters of pastors, bishops and other spiritual leaders, who have been covered up considered an embarrassment to the Church, organization and society. These series of writings were not designed to incite controversy, but to comfort and encourage the illegitimate and unloved "Pastors Kids" to understand that they are relevant, valuable, and important to God. This "Secret Society" is not a secret to God. We can be healed from enforced spiritual leprosy. Our birth had purpose, and our exisitence is one of leadership. This chronicle is an affidavit of the truth, and an insight into the "Life Lessons of a Leader." I salute my mother, who has gone on to glory, for instilling in me faith, courage and strength. Her last words of wisdom were: "Son, help as many people as you can."

Today, I choose to step out of the shadow world full of secrets, lies and cover-ups.

I choose, with the help of God, to assume my true identity and birthright both naturally and spiritually.

Why don't you join me today? Join me in forgiveness, acknowledgement and acceptance of your place in the Kingdom of God as a relevant, successful and fully loved child of God. We can never replace, repair or rectify our isolation, emotional abuse or disowning, but since we are the product of leadership, prove to discontinue this spiritual hypocrisy. I encourage you today to make the choice to live as a true leader in Christ. If there are similarities in my story to yours, know that you are not alone.

Know that the organized church may never welcome or embrace your true identity, for it is filled with personal agendas, hierachy, religious schizophrenia, and dynasty builders.

In the purest form of the Apostolic movement yours may be to blaze a path for God in unchartered, unknown and unrestricted regions that God will assign to your hands thru prayer.

Choose to encourage yourself like King David and re-align your thinking. You have the skills the anointing and the "call" to be a great leader in both spiritual and business matters.

I thank you for investing in your destiny, and for taking the journey to wellness with me.

Wherever you may be serving—the church, the music ministry, local government, politics, retail, etc . . . realize that you are the offspring of greatness and your God is great.

Conclusion of the matter? You are great in the Lord! SELAH! (It is So!)

THE OTHER PULPIT

It's an overcast day and I'm sitting in my favorite local eatery. I just completed another session of teaching music lessons to two of my students at a local church pastored by a good friend. My mind takes me back some 46 years to a Tuesday evening when my life would change forever.

I believe I was playing upstairs in my bedroom, looking forward to a delicious meal, when I heard my mother's high-pitched operatic soprano voice call my name. In 1966 when your parent called for you, you moved immediately if you wanted to live, and I intended to live a long life.

As I hurriedly came running down the spiral staircase, my mother suddenly appeared out of nowhere, and as I got to the last two steps, she stepped up on that step, and towering over me asked me a rhetorical question.

"Do you want to learn how to play the piano?"

I reviewed her request. Even at age 4, I had an analytical mind. I considered my options: a. she cooked all my meals; b. she drove me everywhere in her car; c. she washed all of my clothes; d. I lived in her house rent-free; e. she was way bigger than me. Considering these factors I responded: "Yes ma'am!"

It was at this time, I observed a well-dressed African-American gentleman standing by our baby grand piano, a Chickering model. He would be interrupting my Tuesdays for the next 11 years. His name was Mr. Clarence Bingham. He would teach me more than just classical music. He would teach me leadership skills and become a positive male role model in a fatherless environment.

He instructed me in classical piano training, and was both professional and infinitely patient with his new student.

Each week brought new challenges in learning musical theory, scales, and the classics composed by Beethoven, Brahms and other great composers.

Growing up in an urban neighborhood was a daily challenge within itself, but as I played the classics, I would escape the harshness and poverty.

In my mind, I would travel to France imagining being near the Eiffel Tower. My mother, however, was the real dreamer, who envisioned that her only son would someday play the organ and piano for her gospel choir at the church our family helped to start.

My mother knew a thing or two about starting early in Gospel music. Her pastor who was embarking upon a revolutionary and radical outreach, decided thru prayer, to start a weekly radio broadcast. His selection of radio stations that promoted Gospel, and would accept a Black man for who God created him to be, was very limited.

A beacon of hope began to shine in one of the most unlikeliest of places . . .

In Annapolis, Maryland. The pastor, a man full of faith not fear, followed that star, that led him to the birthplace of slavery in America. Imagine that! It was in this historically racist region that the Christian and Apostolic movement was introduced to Maryland listeners on a weekly basis.

This anointed pastor had received an epiphany. (Sometimes I like to use big collegiate words for validation!) He was to include an anointed choir to be the spiritual jab to his blow of fiery delivery of the Word of God.

Wait a minute! I need to insert this spiritual nugget. In an age of celebrities both in front of and behind the pulpit, many Christian clergy have kissed the feet of Baal, and have taken on a godlike complex, normally associated with medical doctors who've psychologically gone too far.

The Bible states: "The servant is not greater than his master."

The disciples were given an angelic message to "Do greater works," not incorporate greater egos. God get the glory! Christ be lifted up!

You may be asking yourself, "Why'd he go there?" Well, to better give you a clearer outline of the godly character, and quality of church leadership during that time. The point? They were desperate, determined, and zealous to save souls. Not to strategically serve themselves at the expense of both God and His sheep. It was in this atmosphere that I operated and received music instruction.

It was a layered approach. Music lessons on Tuesday, regular and repetitive piano practice after school Monday thru Friday.

Attendance was mandatory at her weekly Saturday rehearals at 5pm. And church all day Sunday. I remember when I was young music wasn't my #1 goal, it was baseball. That's right! I wanted with all my heart to be a baseball player. A Baltimore Oriole. I grew up watching Frank Robinson, Brooks Robinson, Paul Blair, Mark Belanger and Big "Boog" Powell. So I imitated them, created my own baseball teams and league, and had a journal of made-up players with batting averages and different stances for each player. Imagine that?

So I used to play baseball out in front of the church. We had stained-glass windows. I would throw the ball and depending on which groove in the wall it would hit, a different angle and spin would propel the ball out to me. One day I threw the ball too hard and up too high and . . . yeah, you guessed it, I broke the window. Can't tell you the fear and trembling that ran thru my body, and my heart. I accidentally stopped rehearsal. I believe I emptied out the entire church.

My mother was NOT happy. She had to pay for that stained-glass window.

Don't have to tell you that that was the last day I ever played outside.

I had to be kept under constant surveillance from then on and had to sit thru all rehearsals. My punishment became my promotion. It was while watching my mother the choir directress and president, I learned people skills, administration and discipline. Momma was fair but tough as nails when she had to be.

One Saturday, one of the altos questioned why she had selected a certain song for the group to sing. She kept repeating that question as my mother ignored her repeatedly. On the third go round, Momma responded in a clear loud authoritative bellow: "Because I said so!" Here in Maryland, we recently have experienced two hurricanes of note. One of them, Hurricane Irene, had wind swirls of 70-80 mph. The second, Hurricane Sandy, with battering winds of 60-92 mph, didn't hold a candle to the wind gusts associated with that response.

It appeared that the alto's hair blew backwards and she was so shocked she almost fell backwards out of her seat. I was amazed and shocked too. After that, no one said a word for the rest of the rehearsal. I later, with fear and trembling, asked her why she got "gangster" on that alto. She responded quickly: "Niggas will try you and you've got to have an answer ready!" Lesson taught—Never let your choir, praise team, employees, children or even your spouse, challenge your godly authority. So I discovered that this choir I was being groomed to inherit and spiritually chosen to be the minister of music for was created by both vision and obedience.

The pastor of this growing church, approached my grandmother and my mother who was 15 years old, and shared his vision. He challenged them to hear the voice of God thru prayer and recruit talent throughout the church, and form an anointed, fearless group of singing minstrels. Now both Grandma and my mother had some heavy decisions to make. Additionally, my mom's singing talent had also been recognized by the world-famous Caravans.

THE OTHER PULPIT—PART II

The Caravans were a high-energy, super-talented, all-female gospel recording group. Gospel music's version of the Supremes. One of her childhood friends had referred her as a candidate, and she was accepted. However, in those days a parent's voice had power.

My mother was naturally excited. Imagining the possibilities of the glamorous life, being in the recording industry with its national and international travel. Nevertheless, my grandmother prayed too and took her parenting seriously. After much prayer, she came back with an unfavorable decision that would change both my mother's life, the life of her unborn son, and many lives in the Baltimore, Washington, Boston, Philadelphia and New Jersey regions.

My grandmother said "No" to the mighty Caravans. This enraged my mother. She was devastated! Grandma's decision now closed the door to national and international fame and a profitable income. Mother would now have to watch from afar. She now had to buy their LP's like everybody else. It had been decided for her that she could not be famous.

My grandmother followed her faith and the voice of the Lord, and agreed to help this young pastor with his new vision. Essentially, assigning my mother to help him carry out that vision. Helping as an assignment, was not unusual in our family, as it pertains to this particular church. (Leviticus 8:10-12)

The founding pastor had a need to start his ministry, but did not have the money for a church building. It was my great-aunt, we affectionately called Aunt Ilee, who offered the founding pastor her living room to hold weekly worship services at no charge. I'm sure my aunt had an input on my grandma's decision. My immediate family of seven aunts and uncles were all composed of singers and musicians, and had formed their own singing group. They were very active in the city after they arrived from Greenville, S.C., after my grandma separated from my grandfather. I understand that he was a 33rd degree Mason. I met him just once, at my step-grandmother's home in Opelika, Alabama.

So another generation of our family was assigned to build God's church. My mother began recruiting all of her sisters, brothers and talented youth to form this unheard of "Radio Chorus." My mom revealed that as she was entering the radio station on one of their sessions, Pauline Wells Lewis and her sister Sylvia were leaving out. A lifelong friendship would ensue between these pioneering women of Gospel, who made gospel music on the radio a reality.

My mother was very active in the church and that was, it seems, our second home. Imagine church meetings, choir rehearsals and endless church services. It seemed to me that trying to remain holy and sanctified was tough work.

I had a large extended family composed of countless church mothers, who not only adopted me, but kept an organized watchful eye on me.

Let me tell you, it was like a "Church F.B.I." They monitored my clothing, and my whereabouts both in and out of the church.

It was stated that Little Stevie, as I was affectionately called, was so at home being in the church, that I would shake everybody's hands as they passed by for offering. I was told I would stand up on the end pew near the middle aisle, while on the front row, greeting adults like I was the pastor. I was 7 at the time.

I just realized, at age 50, why I was strategically placed on the front row and why I couldn't sit anywhere else. It was so that the network of church mothers, my mother, and my aunts and uncles who made up most of the choir, could keep me under surveillance.

I do recall my very first piano recital. It was held during a Sunday morning service. A keyboard was placed on the rostrum, to the right side of the pulpit.

I actually wished that I could have an out-of-body experience, even at age 7.

Young Master Steven Turner

Listen, this is not your usual stage fright. I mean it's Sunday morning. This is a megachurch of approximately 800-1,000 members. The pastor's about to preach, and I'm doing some kind of classical musical recital instead of a sacred sermonic selection. As I looked around and read the looks on the faces of the congregation, those die-hard members who were traditional in their worship, were saying—as I played Franz List, Hayden and Bethooven—"What in the world is he doing? What in the world is he playing?" Looking at their faces, I could almost read their minds: "Child I don't know what he's doing, but clap and smile anyway. That's Little Stevie." Ah! The church! Birthplace to many super-talented singers, musicians, poets, preachers, etc . . . . The church tolerates undeveloped and the struggling artist. Tell you the truth, you could sound an absolute mess and somebody will clap, pray and give you a hug, when they really should be stoning you to put you out of your misery.

It was somewhere around the 5th grade, that I was allowed to join the choir.

Naturally, I was the youngest member and I was very chubby, but they stuck me out front for some reason, against my will. My momma led this choir, who stood on the rostrum behind the pulpit for 46 years.

Even now, I can remember some of these church-wrecking songs that became the hallmark of the choir's identity. Let me see now . . . alright! Some of them were: "You Must Be Born Again,"

"Footprints of Jesus," and "I've Got Jesus and That's Enough." Well, when I think of that particular selection, I'm reminded of a cold chilly Sunday night. Momma was driving her shiny black Cadillac Seville from our rowhome in West Baltimore, when she suddenly began to pray out loud. I was kinda wondering where this was coming from? She asked God for strength. Now I wasn't a detective, but I gathered from overhearing some of her conversations she'd have with my favorite aunt, that the element of resistance (aka. "haters") who fought against her choir, had tried to discourage her.

So this night she took the rostrum with determination, and when her time came to lead this song, "I've Got Jesus and That's Enough." well . . . OMG!

She bellowed in a clear loud roof-shaking voice: "There's always somebody talking about me!" She paused, squinted her eyes, got all up in the mic and emphasized: "But really I don't mind! They try to stop and block my progress, most of the time!"

"But the mean things you say don't make me feel bad, and I (pause) can't miss a friend that I've never had because . . . (the choir would harmoniously sing) "I've got Jesus and that's enough!" I remember her levitical anointing and power permeated throughout the church, as God came to her rescue, and the Holy Spirit ran thru the church. A shout broke out in the 800-seat sanctuary. Folks began to do 80-yard dashes. I heard loud Baruch-like praises, rhythmic holy dances. Suddenly, my favorite aunt, who always stood beside my mother began to shout and praise God. My momma, always cool, reached out with her right hand, grabbed a hold of her robe so she couldn't fall off the rostrum, as she kept singing from behind the pulpit.

When it was time to sit down, Momma ended the sermonic selection by saying: "I've got Jesus and that's enough!" My God! It was the coolest thing I've ever seen. The church erupted like a volcano all over again, and I believe God danced in Heaven that night.

I was so proud of her! The lesson learned: That as a leader, distractions and dismay delivered like a pizza, will be brought to you by your enemies. The haters of your purpose, anointing and the divine call on your life but you don't have to open the door of your heart to pay for the ungodly pizza that these satanic imps are trying to deliver. Stay true to your destiny, and stay focused in developing into the image of who God has in mind for your life.

You may wonder why I keep referring to certain metaphoric points with food overtures. Well, our family loved food. Let me digress. Church folk love to eat! C'mon now! Let's not get cute!

You know while the pastor, the bishop, nowadays the archbishop and the apostle is preaching, you'd smell the fragrance of that delicious fried chicken, fried fish, smothered pork chops, collard greens, candied yams. Excuse me! Got lost there! You'd be in church saying: "Pastor, how looooong are you gonna keep preaching? A prayer would go up to heaven like: "Dear Lord, Let him end quickly!" Yes, I know! I know! That was wrong and we needed repentance.

Now I know why Christ told Satan, "Man shall not live by bread alone." Should've said fried chicken, the "Gospel Bird," mascot of the Black Church. I apologize for that light-hearted parody, but humor was big in our house, and in my relationship with my late mother.

I recall a beautiful and bright Sunday afternoon as my mother and I returned from morning service.

We had stopped at Ginos now known as KFC and purchased a bucket of the Colonel's best Southern fried chicken. We exited our vehicle, a 1979 Cadillac Sedan DeVille, with the unmistakeable fragrance of those 11 herbs and spices. If I'm not mistaken, she had on a pearly white usher's uniform. Yes, my momma ushered during the morning, and was a choir directress at night. As I recall, she was especially happy that day, and began to walk up the steps to our home. Now, ushers are supposed

to be light on their feet. I'm not sure whether the smell of the golden brown fried chicken, or the eagerness to eat it got the best of her, but as I walked ahead of her I heard, "Oh!" I suddenly turned around holding the ice-cold sodas, and I saw my momma laying on the ground. Now I wondered if she was still in the Spirit laying prostrate, like the prophets, in worship? However, I quickly dismissed that 'cause church was over. Let me slow this down . . . .

She had fallen going up the side steps. Why? Instead of taking the next set of steps, trying to hurry up and eat, she took a shortcut up the hill in her pearly white usher shoes. Now these church shoes were not built for off-terrain, SUV-walking. So when she fell forward, the golden crispy fried chicken with all those 11 herbs and spices fell out and rolled like cattle down the hill in the dirt. You can't hear me, but I'm being transformed back to that moment, and I am laughing as hard as I laughed then.

I immediately yelled out while moving to where she laid flat on the ground and said, "Momma are you ok?" She responded, "Yes!" I said, "Well, I guess we'll have to eat something else now that the chicken has rolled down the hill and gotten dirty." She immediately looked up at me with fiery determination, lowered her voice and said: "Child, I paid good money for this chicken, and I'm going to eat my chicken!" So we went in the house laughing. Her uniform was dirty, the chicken was dirty, but we blew the dirt off and ate it anyway. Yes, we violated the three-second rule, but we were poor and had to be resourceful to survive. In spite of the laughter, there was a "Life Lesson" here as well. All of us had an original purpose allocated to us by God. We may have been dropped, gotten dirty from making some bad choices that's caused us pain, but God sent somebody along to blow the dirt off of our lives, off of our gifts, off of our vision, off of our damaged low self-esteem. Helped us to our feet, and said, as we were being helped up, that God still intends to use you for the original purpose that you were put here for. Scripture tells us that our righteousness in its glory is still nothing but filthy rags. So it's alright! That affair! That cocaine! That unearned promotion!

That crime did not disinherit you from the Kingdom of God. Just repent and ask God to lead you back to the road of your destiny in Him. Now that's good news! (If the joy of the Lord has begun to break out and the tears of joy are flowing, take a praise break. Hallelujah!)

This is the home we lived in together for 34 years.

THE OTHER PULPIT

Life Lesson— Limit Your Untouchable Heros

Whenever I hear the words "Good News" I think of God's Holy Word and my thoughts turn immediately to my father. He was my hero! The best preacher I've EVER heard. Considered by many of his contemporaries to be a "Preacher's Preacher". My mind races back to a cloudy and overcast Monday morning. I was playing "Church" in my bedroom upstairs on the second floor in the rear bedroom overlooking the back yard. My bedroom was located next to the bathroom down a long hallway which separated me from my momma's bedroom. We were poor, so toys were at a premium.

I adapted and improvised and had made a pulpit out of a steel milk crate. Yes I used a makeshift pulpit. I began to emulate my father as he preached. He had delivered an exceptionally furious sermon that had set the church on fire. I was both elated and extremely proud. I longed to tell him, but I could not. He was unavailable. So, in my subconscious mind, I internalized and mentally tape recorded from afar my hero, my father's sermon. As I mimicked his actions and mirrored his voice patterns, something came over me. Today, I recognize it was the Holy Ghost. I began to walk down the hall, made a right passed the steps and into my mother's bedroom. She was in bed, talking on the telephone. I drew on heavenly strength, narrowed my eyes, raired back and declared with power: "Momma! I'm going to preach!" It was stated with passion. I then left the room almost as immediately as I came, returned to my bedroom and became a child again. My mother, however, never forgot that day, and thought about it until the day she died.

Life Lesson— Differences Dress You For Your Destiny

I wanted desperately to be like the other kids in our neighborhood. I had to wear a dress shirt, neckties, and dress pants to school everyday. I wore glasses, and I was fat. Making matters worst, I couldn't grow a bush (afro). So by those standards I was not cool. I was immediately identified, on the first day of school, as if I thought I was better than everybody else. Not true, but the bullying and harassment would continue because of the way people interpreted my style of dress. It's a shame that an eye for fashion is discouraged, and as my mother instilled the value of having a good appearance is so competitive, even in the church. I remember a Sunday morning worship service at a local church where I was serving as the minister of music. The pastor approached me and said, "What are you trying to do? Look better than the pastor?" I was amazed! What was I wearing, you ask? It was a two-piece separate, a red suit with red / gold suede shoes. Leadership Lesson—Scripture: "Man looks on the outside, but God looks at the heart." Jealousy is an untimely and unwelcomed hindrance to success and unity. The Bible states that "Jealousy is crueler than the grave."

At some point during my teen years, I was drafted to sing lead on a song entitled "Sign Me Up" by the J.C. White Singers. As I entered our warm-up rehearsal every Sunday night before singing for weekly radio broadcast, my mother announced that shocking piece of news. The closer my Sunday to sing came the more nervous I got. Finally, the day came I dreaded, and as I took the rostrum, along with my mother's choir, it seemed that the church was packed, even in the balconies. The music intro was being played and I was petrified. How did I handle that? Well . . . I didn't move a muscle when it came time to sing. I didn't move the second time as the pianist and organist played the intro.

I was beginning to think I could get away with it a third time and not sing at all, when my mother angrily stepped forward and fanned me with her hand out of the chorus of singers. I was ordered to get to the microphone behind the pulpit. Laziness and apathy were not allowed on her watch. So I began to sing the lead. It was to me terrible, because I didn't have formal voice lessons as I had on the piano. It came out all nasally like those dwarfs who sing "Follow the yellow brick road" in the "Wizard of Oz."

This delighted the pastor's daughter who played the organ and directed the youth mass choir. They all began to laugh out loud as I struggled. When the song was over, I was so embarrassed, that I kept my head down in shame. I ran out and hid in the church bathroom. My mother was a great singer, all of my aunts and uncles could sing well. 'Dear Lord,' I asked, 'what happened to me?' After we would sing for the broadcast, the taped recordings of that service would be delivered to the radio station where it would be played all over the state. That radio broadcast would come on every Saturday at noon. The choir would sing their signature theme song. They sang their first selection. It went well.

Then came my song. I was nervous, excited and extremely insecure, and when I heard myself for the very first time, I hated it. It was so bad, I actually ran from the kitchen on the first floor of our home, all the way upstairs to the attic on the third floor to hide out. I refused to come down, and my mother continued to laugh at me, promising me, "You'll get better after awhile, son." Mom's telephone began to ring off the hook as church members and friends called to congratulate her. I was horrified, stunned, and wanted no more of singing of any kind. The next time I sang, I got the same results.

Only this time, the youth choir, directed by the pastor's daughter, began to laugh out loud as soon as they heard the intro music for my song. It was doubly humiliating and I begged my mother to find someone else to lead that song. She replied, "You're going to sing lead! So don't focus on negativity!"

She further advised singing tips: "Son, focus on a friendly face or look at one of the light fixtures that hang in the ceiling above." As much as I dreaded it, it became time to sing that song again.

An overwhelming dread came over me, and as I went to the bathroom to hide out again, something happened. It was there that I looked in the mirror, and asked God would He bless me to release blessings on His people. I washed my face and prayed each step leading to the pulpit. The organist and pianist played the intro to my song as usual. The youth choir began to laugh out loud as usual also.

Suddenly, I felt an unusual spirit of peace calming me down. I stepped up to the microphone and stood behind the pulpit, opened my mouth and began to sing. To my, and everyone else's sudden amazement, my voice became strong, heavy and powerful. People began to jump up, clap, praise, shout and hug each other. Life Lesson—When leaders take the focus off themselves, and are more concerned with blessing God's sheep, God will respond and answer your prayers. Finally, when you place God's desires, His purpose and plans for your life first, miracles can now enter the Earth.

THE OTHER PULPIT

Life Lesson— The DNA Of A Leader Is Recognizable By Others

As a child, I recall the night of 1968. I was 4 years old. I remember the civil alarms sounding, and the curfew being enforced. My mother and I were out shopping, and had to hurry home before the National Guard took over the city, with a shoot to kill order approved by the mayor and governor.

Our business district, just 2 blocks away, had been looted and destroyed in the riots following the assassination of Dr. Martin Luther King. As the intensity of these events hit home, my mother began to cry.

Later on in life, I would discover that she had actually met the famed civil rights leader personally at a civil rights event held at a local church. Fascinated, I listened intently as she described their chance meeting. She stated: "That Dr. King delivered a powerful preached message, and was heavily anointed, a prophet sent by God." She further commented: "His eyes were so intense, that it seemed as if he was looking right thru you!" Amazingly, I had been told the same thing. One summer afternoon, as I played street football with my cousins on the Eastside, while walking up my aunt's white marble steps, I turned to look at one of my new friends I'd been playing with. He covered his face and yelled: "Don't look at me like that!" I asked, 'Why?' He replied, "Your eyes! It's like you're looking right through me!" I never forgot that day. My mother kept a tri-fold picture frame in her den area. It contained just 3 photos. One was of Dr. Martin Luther King, the other was of my father, and the third was . . . of me. I always wondered what I was doing among such spiritual giants who had gained local, regional, national and international success and accolades.

THE OTHER PULPIT

Life Lesson—Destiny Is Not Microwaveable

I believed that God revealed to my momma my ultimate purpose, and the plans He's made for my life, before He took her home. Perhaps that's why she was so protective and always operated with me in a training mode. Subsequently, this is why being a trainer comes so easily to me. As a future minister of music, I was always in training.

My mother trained me constantly at home, running out of the kitchen; thru the dining room to where the organ was in the living room. She was preparing lunch or dinner, heard something wrong, and would come running and teaching whenever I hit a bad chord, played too loud – or worse – too fast!

Somedays it seemed as if she had skates on, and truthfully, I would be extremely irritated, because I thought I was all that. Mother would bust my bubble by letting me know I had a long way to go.

Lesson learned—God honors and appreciates humility. To be a student in both music and in life, one must be both meek and humble. To be a leader he must be an effective student. Talking while the teacher is instructing is counter-productive and arrogant.

God assigns, makes, and distributes ministers of music, music prophets and minstrels to suit His purpose and for His glory. We can emulate, copy successful and talented leaders in an industry. However, industry is *not* ministry. The goals and purpose are not the same. One is self-made, and the other is God-made. The scripture advises: "The humble shall be exalted and the meek shall inherit the Earth." We never have to be spiritually pushy; it is written that a man's gift will make room for him. The problem is we don't want to wait on our ministry, as if we can speed up God's clock. Let patience have her perfect work. God will release that regional, national and even international ministry when you are spiritually, mentally and emotionally ready. Enjoy the downtime now, while you study and show yourself approved. The days will come when you may wish you had waited a little longer.

THE OTHER PULPIT

Life Lesson—
Be Persistently Humble

I wasn't allowed to continue after 11 years in classical music studies, although it was foundationally great training. However, there is an air of aristocracy and politics that flow thru it. The church I was born into and a member of, didn't understand or like it, even though I was afforded an opportunity by the pastor to do those recitals.

Even on his rostrum. Even at a young age, I saw and sensed the resistance and toleration of my development. I complained to my mother that I no longer wanted to play, and protested by going on strike, refusing to play for an entire year.

She began to search for a teacher to train me to play by ear.

This dissatisfaction came about while seated at the piano before an evening service. One of my musician friends pulled my sheet music away and said, "Play it again by ear." I became intimidated and frustrated as pride took over and I became embarrassed that I didn't have a clue what to do next. I wanted to take lessons from a retail music store, but after awhile, the commercial environment could not train me in the realm of anointed playing.

So, I became bored and stopped playing. I tried to go on strike and quit; however, my mother and my future employer, would not allow it. No matter how hard I kicked against the pricks!

THE OTHER PULPIT

Life Lesson—
Parents Ensure Godly Gender Hood. Raise Your King David.

There was no male role model to emulate in our home, so my mother took me down to our church, and signed me over to the deacons, who were also Boy Scout leaders. She requested them to ensure that I would develop into a good man, learn to follow good leadership, and participate with others. These were godly men that I both respected and looked up to, who also respected my mother as a godly woman. They taught me not only humility, but also how to use faith in not backing down from challenges you might face in life. Case in point, on a chilly Saturday afternoon on a ballfield behind the church, we were playing flag football, but couldn't afford any flags.

I was selected for a team, and spent time playing on both offense and defense. I remember it well. At the close of the game, we were losing and one of the oldest boys on the opposing team had the ball. He ran thru our defense, like a hot knife thru melted butter. He was on his way for the game-winning touchdown again. Only one thing stood in his way . . . me. Let me describe this. He was 5ft. 9in, 175 lbs. approximately, with full facial hair, a "bad-boy" reputation and a bad attitude to match. I was "David" at 4ft. 7in., 105 lbs. soaking wet, bald as an eagle, and a certified "Momma's Boy" (OMG!) I thought, 'Let him run it in for a touchdown! He's too big and mean to even think about trying to physically tackle him.'

However, like David, courage sprung up, like a well of water, and I began to run fast towards him. He had the end zone on his mind, so he never saw me coming from an angle. I outran him, and as I got close, I leaped up in the air and threw my 105 lbs. into his left shoulder and side, knocking him off balance.

He fell and dropped the football. I immediately picked it up and ran the opposite way into the end zone for the game-winning touchdown, as the whole field looked on in amazement. When this modern-day Goliath got to his feet, and realized that the smallest and youngest player on the field had taken him down, he became embarrassed and full of pride. He wanted to fight me and had to be restrained by the Boy Scout church deacons. Members of both teams lifted me up on their shoulders and paraded me around the field. Humility and courage are compatible when allowed to be used by God. We overcome our biggest adversaries using the faith and courage that's within us. I've discovered from a former pastor fluent in Hebraic studies that the Hebrew definition of faith is "emunah." "Emunah" as we're taught, is the total blind faith that a child has in believing that their father, mother or nowadays, grandma, is going to do what they promised. It is the total obedience to instruction given.

The children of Israel grew tired of waiting to see the Promised Land and believing in a God who operated in clouds and a pillar of fire.

They eventually erected a golden calf on an altar because godly leadership had stayed away too long.

THE OTHER PULPIT

Life Lesson—Obedience vs Sacrifice

My first music instrument I wanted to play was not the keyboard, but the drums. Back in my day public schools taught music education as a curriculum. (Bring it back!) So in elementary school, I became interested and excited about becoming a drummer. However, my mother did not share my enthusiasm, stating I made too much noise. Imagine it! I was banging and beating on everything including the kitchen sink. Ha-ha! Maybe that was her motivation for leading me to the acoustic piano to learn the foundational theory thru classical music. The long hours of practice, learning scales, notes sight-reading, while being forced to be disciplined.

I couldn't go out as the other kids in the neighborhood, until my homework and music studies were completed. I remember only once Mom allowed me to go out and play before my music practice.

I'd thought I'd gotten away completely from having to practice, because she didn't say anything about it. I did my homework, watched TV, ate dinner, watched more TV. I became sleepy and went to bed.

She began to call my name. I immediately responded, slightly annoyed (You've been there, haven't you?) I said, "Ma'am!" She looked me up and down as I responded downstairs in my pajamas in the hallway. "You forgot that you had to practice?" she asked. "I told you if I let you go outside to play with your friends, you would have to practice when you came back in didn't I?"

I began to be nervous! "Momma," I said in my 'I'm your only son' voice, "it's after 11:30 pm."

She quickly responded. "I don't care how late it is, you're going to keep your word." Lesson learned, as I begrudgingly went to the piano in anger—Whatever you promise, you'd better keep your end of the bargain. She was teaching me to have a godly character and be reliable.

She faithfully led the Gospel Recording Choir for over 40 years. She never missed a Sunday service.

This unrelentless pursuit of excellence was the hallmark of our home that God reigned over.

THE OTHER PULPIT

Life Lesson—Yield Not To Temptation

When I wasn't practicing my daily piano exercises, I still had to live in the real world outside of the church. School #67, my elementary school, had a world of memories, triumphs, and challenges.

On the night before school, my mother, a nurse, drove me from home to my new school. This type of reconnaissance was to train me on memorization thru repetitive actions.

You might think I'm talking about chord structures and scale or tonal components. Nevertheless, I'm referring to following directions, and learning obedience. My mother was intent on preparing my mind to think outside the box, and to be a leader who dared to be different. How, you might ask?

So glad you did! She would send me to school alone on the pre-recorded preferred path of travel, and I would arrive to school dressed in a suit and tie, pants and dress shoes, as if I was running a company or pastoring some church. Now I did say we lived in the ghetto right? Soooo . . . other kids, especially on the first day of school, would be gathered outside, looking at me like, "Who does this negro think he is?" "He must think he's better than us!" Translation: I was put on the "hit" list to be abused and bullied, even before I could get in the front door. They called me names like "Preacher Man," "Reverend," "Big-head, necktie wearing . . . ." I soon got tired of this bullying and unwanted attention.

I tried to take matters into my own hands, even at age 6 and 7. How? By wearing another shirt under my shirt and tie Momma laid out for me to wear to school. Why? So I could be cool and fit in with everybody else. One day she asked me, "Are you wearing your shirt and tie to school?"

I said, "Yes Ma'am!" She then asked for some reason: "Are you walking the route I told you to walk?" I shortened my answer to "Yes Ma'am!" I didn't know that this was part of her quality control procedure. You know they have in manufacturing and telephone outbound calling where a supervisor has to verify your sale? Same methodology (Got that word from my wife, felt like throwing it around). I was being set-up people. Had too much to worry about to recognize it and here's why. The biggest student at school hated my guts, because I was small, had a big head, big forehead, talked extremely fast, flat chested, and wore shirts and ties to class everyday. Piece of work huh? He – Mr. Perfect – was tall, cool and looked like a grown man. Why? He had been kept back a few times, and had begun to use his father's razor to shave his beard. (Lol! I needed that!) One day, after eating a marvelous lunch, a friend and I sat on the back row of the auditorium talking.

The bully came from my right shoulder, yelling hateful comments and threatening my life. The usual day-to-day drama. He was eating cake, and he took that cake in his right hand and smashed it in the top of my head. Not satisfied, he then rubbed it in. Everybody laughed. I was, I felt, powerless because he was so big and I was more afraid of dying if I objected. Suddenly, I heard a sweet voice telling him to stop. Who would dare? I was amazed! I turned and saw this tall, very attractive woman who had long pigtails like an Indian, defending me. Well . . . I was the happiest cake-wearing dude that ever lived. She walked me back to class, after getting all of the cake out of my hair. Yes, what you're thinking is true. We became an item. She being "Beauty" seemed to be the only person who could control her brother, "The Beast." So one day she asked me if she could walk me home and wanted to take a short cut. I immediately responded like a P.O.W. and said "I'm only supposed to walk down North Avenue only." She said sweetly, "Who told you that?" I nervously responded, "My momma." She said: "I thought you were a man who made his own decisions?" She was leaning so close to me, all in my eyes, that I was thinking I would get my first ever in life . . . kiss! I said, "Uhm! Yes! Yes! I can go with you to take the shortcut," and so I did. (Sounded like the conversation between Eve and the Serpent.) We were arm in arm walking down this new path. Imagine! Shaving off time, beating red lights.

The air seemed cleaner, the sun brighter, I stuck my chest out. I was walking with this gorgeous, taller older woman. People looked at me like I was the man. WOW! She was right. I had just made a manly decision. Life was great! Like the Prophet Moses, I could see the Promised Land. We were about a half block away from my street, when suddenly the air got thick, the sun stopped shining, the concrete under my feet began to buckle. Was this an earthquake? A military attack? The Rapture? I heard a heavy sound to my left behind me. I knew that sound instantly. The Bible quotes Christ as saying: "My sheep know My voice and a stranger they will not follow. We can expand that to include the motor of my momma's car.

Now I had never been in the military so I don't know how I learned this defensive and evasive military maneuver, but I dropped to the ground. I was parallel to a parked car, hoping it would hide me. (I was humming the song: "He shall hide me!"). I told my beautiful date to keep on walking, that my mother was behind us. I said a prayer:

"Dear God in Heaven! Let this cup pass, and let, I pray, me become invisible!"

Selah! (Never knew Christ prayed a similar prayer in the Garden of Gethsemane.)

My mother pulled up between the parked cars and said very calmly: "You can get up off the ground, and come on home. Your backside belongs to me," and drove off.

I began to sing a Negro spiritual and cry thinking about the pain on the horizon.

I blamed my date for tempting me to do wrong. She said, "I didn't force you to come with me" and left me there to die y'all!

Your temptors are *not* your friends and are the sub-agents of Satan.

The Bible further states, "The tender mercies of the wicked are cruel."

Temptations start off reasonable and logical, and may be even practical.

It's so appealing, resolutional, and immensely satisfying, as it leads you happily to your death.

Be determined that YOU shall not die but live!!!

THE OTHER PULPIT

Life Lesson—The Strap Sermon

Yes people, I got the beating of my life. Momma kept her promise, as she delivered a sermon that afternoon. Although she never went to seminary, she delivered a powerful message of obedience to my "rearguard". I remember it well, it went something like this: "This will (Ha!) hurt me more (Hold the note!) than it will you! (Note: Modern scientific research in pain management have proven this point to be untrue.)

"I told you (Ha!) not to go down any other paths, but the one I told you to go! And, and, and I meant what I said! (Oh Lord!) But you didn't listen!

She had the amazing spiritual gift to both ask a question and answer it all at the same time.

Mothers, it appeared, were the original developers of multi-tasking. She continued. "You *will* do what I say won't you?!" This sermon was backed by the melodic and well-timed right hand overtures of a thick black leather belt. When the Spirit entered my body I said "YES," and began to dance not for joy, but to stay alive. I prayed to God that I'd never have to go thru this fiery test again.

However, it became an annual event whenever I messed up in a new area.

Nevertheless, the real lesson learned—"Walk the path that has been purposed by God for your life."

Don't let any man, woman, employer, church, neighborhood association, hobby or addiction, get you off that path that God has chosen for your life.

Get up off that couch! That office desk! That gutter! Break the bars of low self-esteem, and ask God to show you and keep you on the path of hope, joy, and righteousness,

Know that you are made in HIS image!

You are valuable!

Be the blessing that GOD wants you to be!

THE OTHER PULPIT

Life Lesson—Determine What Pulpit to Stand Behind

As I close this segment, I want to thank you for taking the journey with me. My mother envisioned me behind the pulpit, leading a congregation, and winning mass souls for the Kingdom of God. I've discovered that God has many pulpits that He allows the called and the chosen to preach the Word from. Many theologians and organized clergy will reference the traditional wooden or polymer-plastic pulpit on the rostrum that has now become more of a stage. Televised performances seem to make celebrities out of the persons behind it. However, Christ when He walked the earth (Emmanuel) among us, never paraded His titles in front of us, like we do to gain status, popularity, ratings, and money. So in the same spirit of Christ, I declare in your hearing today that there is another pulpit. This pulpit is less appreciated. Why more church budgetary monies are spent on its upkeep than the modern-day Levite, who with God's help, must bring it to life weekly.

Faithfully, toiling, leading, teaching and serving in an atmosphere of disrespect, under- and non-appreciation, abuse, hostility and slave-like working conditions. For this cause I was put on the earth? Yes! To this ministry was I called and chosen for. To use the universal language of music, mentioned 989 times in the Holy Bible. To heal the broken hearted. Psalms is the longest book in the Bible. To give recovering of sight to the blind. Preachers preach in musical keys found on the keyboard. To heal them that are bruised. Prophets couldn't prophecy without a minstrel (music prophet) To preach the acceptable year of the Lord. Christ (Logos) will have only singing and music in Heaven. What an honor to be a minstrel, psalmist, minister of music or music prophet! Power is given thru annointed music to tear down demonic strongholds, expose and dismantle political policies and procedures that choke both the Word and the sheep. Now unto every minister of music, psalmist, bass player, drummer, congo player, keyboard player, lead / rhthym guitar player, music producer and engineer, songwriter, arranger: This is your year to "Preach the acceptable year of the Lord."

THE OTHER PULPIT

Life Lesson— Play Loud! Cry Loud! Your Gift is Making Room.

The conclusion of the matter is: As my last teacher announced to my surprise that he was releasing me, I thought it was due to some failure on my part. That he was rejecting me from continuance as his student. He revealed that when I first arrived 4 years earlier, I was so bad as a music student, that he contemplated calling my mother and refunding not some, but all of the money she had spent.

Wow! That was a devastating moment to realize you were just that bad.

Nevertheless, he quickly added that the real reason why he can no longer keep me as his student was that I had learned everything he knew, and had no more he could teach me. He stated that he was proud of me. Due to my diligent and persistence I had now surpassed all of his music students.

His next words were shocking to me: "Therefore, I now release you to the world."

Later on I would hear a similar recitation coming from a dear friend who was closing his church where I had served as his minister of music. He said with tears in his eyes when I asked "What do I do now?"

He replied, "I release you to the world as a universal minister of music." I was astonished.

It has taken many years, and thru much pain, and the sacrifice of others to finally emerge into this prophecy. I can assure you when others say I should be retiring from the ministry, that I am just spiritually waking up and accepting my destiny from God. You don't have to spiritually procrastinate. I feel like Apostle Paul now. So as an Apostle of Music I release every Musician, Psalmist and Levite to go forth from the Hammond B3, Korg Trition and acoustic piano.

Be thou released for it is time "TO SING A NEW SONG!"

Do it from "The Other Pulpit" that God holds so dear!

Keep your heads up and stand strong!

Printed in the United States
By Bookmasters